Mel Bay presents

# JAZZ GUITAR ETUDES

### by Alan de Mause

D1452294

**INTRODUCING CONCEPTS AND TECHNIQUES OF FINGERSTYLE SOLO JAZZ GUITAR, FOR FLAT PICK PLAYERS WITH LITTLE OR NO PREVIOUS FINGERSTYLE EXPERIENCE**

**DEDICATION:**
To Alfie Mc Court, Ernesto Beltrez, and all the staff at the Los Panchos Restaurant, who heard me working this out in public for two and a half years.

**THANKS TO:**
Bill Bay, for suggesting the need for this book and once again bringing you and me together.

Christine Sotmary, and Jordan Myers for help with typing and Mark Lonergan for proof-reading.

Jim Hall, Jimmy Raney, Johnny Smith, and George Van Eps for being the inspiration they have been to me for so many years. When I read through the etudes in this book I see them waving at me.

Jimmy Wyble, whose solo jazz guitar playing is ingenious, delightful, and a shining example of less-is-more.

Kathleen Adkins, Werner Erhard, and all of the people who have participated with me throughout the years at the New York Area Center. This book, beyond my ego, is from you, too, and for all.

**ACKNOWLEDGEMENTS TO:**
Master tape for optional cassette recorded at Lobel Productions, West New York, New Jersey, and the studio of Marilyn Ries, New York City, New York

Photography, unless otherwise credited, by Michael Ian, New York City, New York

The flat top seven string guitar shown in many of the photographs was built by Miguel Luciano, New York City, New York

Cassette available from the store where you purchased this book.

Cover photo by Michael Ian

# ABOUT THE AUTHOR

Author Alan de Mause is a veteran of Broadway shows, big bands, record dates and the club world. Currently he teaches at Columbia University and in his own Manhattan studio. Besides specializing in unaccompanied solo jazz guitar, he concertizes with *A Small Circle of Friends.* In addition to music, Alan does announcing and voice-overs, and recently completed a series of exercise records for the Gateway label.

When not playing, writing, or teaching music, he is involved with the World Runners' Club, the World Hunger Project, and the New York Area Center. His pursuits include Chinese cooking, yoga, and Zen.

> "My fate as a guitarist was sealed when I was thirteen. Roy Rogers, on a promotional tour through my home city of Detroit, shook my hand. I decided if I could only play guitar like Roy, anything was possible. My parents might even buy me a horse like Trigger. Well, now I can play *even better* than Roy. I'm still waiting for the horse."
>
> message from an interview with author

# INTRODUCTION

**That you even *know* about unaccompanied solo jazz guitar ...**
Not so many years ago if you asked the average guitarist to name his favorite finger-style solo jazz guitarist, he would have been hard put to name one, much less a favorite. Soloists existed, of course, but the form was not as popular as other forms of guitar playing. Today? Joe Pass, Ralph Towner, George Van Eps. Lenny Breau, Ted Greene, Jimmy Wyble, Bucky Pizzarelli, Larry Coryell, Charlie Byrd, to name only a few, are known, have a following of imitators, and play every kind of jazz from swing and bop through every kind of fusion.

**Come on in, the water's fine**
I specifically mentioned Joe Pass first. After a successful career playing in groups he courageously jumped into the solo pond and started paddling with his pick, and only minimal fingerstyle as a backup life preserver. The prevailing opinion that one couldn't play solo jazz guitar without the fingerstyle technique of Segovia didn't seem to bother him.

Don't let it bother you, either. *And,* gaining some fingerstyle technique is a big part of what this book is about. The ability you have now in playing jazz with a pick, your ability to read music, and courage and patience with yourself is all you need to become a fingerstyle solo jazz guitarist.

**Solo jazz guitar—and more**
"I love all that fingery stuff on jazz guitar! Let me at it! How do I get all of that going —just what is the fingerstyle approach?"

"I play in groups on club dates and dances. When there is no pianist, I am asked to play solo guitar during the band breaks. I have known and lived with panic and fear. Help!"

"I back up singers. When I am with a group, I can play lead or rhythm, or little figures, but when I replace a pianist as the only accompanist, what I do is too thin-sounding. How can I flesh it out?"

"I hear guitarists 'comp' behind their own playing. How is that done?"

...and on and on. Virtually any artistic or commercial situation you would find yourself in would be enhanced by your knowledge of a self-accompanied fingerstyle solo approach.

***Jazz Etudes:* de-mystifying the art of self-accompanied solo jazz guitar**
At first hearing, fingerstyle solo jazz guitar can be more than a little overwhelming. Melding together are improvised lead lines *and* chordal work *and* bass lines *and* rhythmics.

Relax. Since you already play jazz with a pick, you *are* familiar with many of the musical elements used in fingerstyle jazz. It's just that it may not be obvious to you what, specifically, fingerstyle *concepts* and *techniques* are. That's exactly where this book begins.

The jazz etudes in Part One of this book are for pick *or* fingerstyle solo jazz guitar. Each etude illustrates a specific self-accompanying device. Gradually, *fingerstyle technique* is introduced along with the *concepts* used in fingerstyle solo playing. Techniques and concepts of fingerstyle jazz will enable you to start *thinking* fingerstyle.

Part Two is for fingerstyle *only,* illustrating the techniques and concepts unique to the mode.

Part Three consists of several full-blown arrangements, using all of the techniques and concepts presented in the book.

The etudes are either original tunes or "improvised" choruses on standard tunes, identified as such. I have purposely used the latter method so that you can relate this material to tunes and chord progressions you already know.

Supplemental source material is mentioned throughout the book, and I encourage you to use it—especially if fingerstyle playing is new for you. Technique won't come in one etude's worth of work.

## What this project needs is you

Until recently, the art of playing jazz was considered too mysterious to be captured in print. Now, every aspect of jazz guitar has been transcribed, analyzed, divided, organized, presented in order of difficulty, printed and bound, and is sold at your nearest music store. And here we are: you and this book, through Mel Bay Publishing and me.

It *might* seem as though I've done a lot of work *for* you—and, sometimes, as a writer, I wonder if I have stolen your learning experience. Both impressions are false, since here this book sits, silent, full of directions and symbols. No music is in the air yet. Having purchased this book is not the same as personally owning the knowledge inside or using the contents in your daily guitar life.

In the age of the information explosion, old fashioned work still is the only thing that—works.

Make yourself proud of yourself. If you truly want to learn to play fingerstyle solo jazz guitar, then *use* this book. Wear out the pages before you buy the next one.

Aspen, Colorado, 1971                                              Photo by Arabella Simon

4

# PART ONE: PLAYING SOLO JAZZ GUITAR WITH THE FLAT PICK WHILE ADDING FINGERSTYLE TECHNIQUE

# PART TWO: CONCEPTS AND TECHNIQUES UNIQUE TO FINGERSTYLE GUITAR

# PART THREE: ALL THINGS CONSIDERED, COMBINING ALL OF THE CONCEPTS AND TECHNIQUES INTRODUCED

# PART ONE: PLAYING WITH THE FLAT PICK WHILE ADDING FINGERSTYLE TECHNIQUE

| | |
|---|---|
| **Etude One:** | *Pick a Simple Tune* |
| **Concept:** | Delineating chord changes with a continuous, single note, melodic line |
| **Technique:** | Right hand: a) flat pick: normal technique used in scales and close voiced arpeggiation<br>b) fingerstyle: alternate index-middle, rest stroke<br>Left hand: normal (pick style) technique |

## Don't drop your pick

Solo guitar *is* solo guitar, whether you play it with your fingers, your pick,—or your foot. There are players who can play a whole lot of solo guitar with a pick, such as Al DiMeola, Larry Coryell, Joe Pass, and others. Anything and everything you have learned with the pick you can include in your finger-style playing, and for a while, at least, you may want to switch back and forth.

## Single note lines in unaccompanied soloing

The familiar pick-style single note lead line *is* part of solo guitar playing. After all, instruments such as brass or woodwind instruments play only one note at a time, and do play unaccompanied solos. As long as a single note solo line is *complete in content*, it can serve as an unaccompanied solo. What I mean by that will be explained after you play the solo below. It is an improvisation based on eight measures of a familiar chord progression\*, played twice through. Play it with your pick.

\*Part of many jazz standards, including *When the Saints Go Marching In, The Nearness of You, Cherokee, If I Had You, I May Be Wrong* and *God Bless the Child*

## Completeness of content

To make your single-line solos sound complete-unto-themselves, pay attention to both the *rhythmic flow* and the *choice of notes* you use.

1. *The note flow should be almost constant.* The eighth note is the basic rhythmic unit of traditional jazz soloing, and using it keeps the jazz pulse going. Use other note values for variety, of course, but avoid long rests...unless you want to stamp your foot loudly in order to remind your listeners that the solo is still going! Remember, you are the whole band, and when you stop, the music stops.

2. *Your choice of notes must delineate the chord progression.* When you play with a group, more than likely there is another guitarist or a keyboard player to back you in your single line solos. Whatever you play, your accompanist is still tracking the basic harmony of the piece. In unaccompanied solo guitar, you are *It*, alone, and in order to show the harmonic underpinnings of the piece you have to do it with your choice of notes. This is especially true in single-note-only sections of your solo. Use crucial chord tones, and stay away from one tone or blues-scale-only solos.

   Examine *Pick a Simple Tune* for rhythmic flow and see how the note selection indicates the chord progression.

## Playing linear material fingerstyle

By *linear material* I mean passages which are basically scale-like, in up-and-down-the-hill movements, chromatic movement, closely-spaced arpeggiation, and only an occasional large intervallic leap. The notes lie mostly on adjacent strings. The above solo is an example of linear material.

In fingerstyle guitar, linear material when unaccompanied is played primarily with the index and middle fingers (*i-m*) of the right hand, in alternation, using a *rest stroke.*

## First steps in fingerstyle guitar: position

First, you might need to adjust the position of your guitar for fingerstyle playing. In the traditional classical guitar position, the guitar is *centered* in relation to the body. Any position which approximates this is fine.

11

With the guitar centered in relation to your body, place the right forearm on the side of the guitar (not the face) and let the wrist loosely hang free. Place the first three fingers of the right hand on the first string. On any other string temporarily place your thumb well away from the fingers in a sort of inverted hitch-hiking position. When this is done correctly, there is a triangle of space between the thumb and index finger and the *i, m* and *a* fingers are in line on the same plane.

| Right hand fingers | |
| --- | --- |
| Thumb | p |
| Index | i |
| Middle | m |
| Ring | a |
| Pinkie | e* |

*The little finger (e) is sometimes used for chord or arpeggio work, in which case it must be lowered by twisting the hand somewhat.

**The rest stroke (also called accent stroke, leaning stroke, appoyando)**

The *rest stroke* is used primarily for *emphasizing* or producing volume. When you wish the melody to stand out, use the rest stroke. Here's how to do it. Temporarily move the thumb and rest it on the sixth string for support. Place the *i* finger on the first string and raise the *m* and *a* fingers away from the first string. Now pluck the first string with the *left side* of the fingertip (as you look at it from underneath the hand) and nail of the *i* finger and *come to rest on the second string*, letting the first segment of the finger and tip give a little. Don't keep it frozen in position.

Now, and forever after, begin the stroke *in front of* the string to be sounded, striking the string as the finger is moving, midstroke. Henceforth, resting the finger on the string to be plucked is *verboten*, as doing this would cut short any still-ringing note just plucked on that string.

 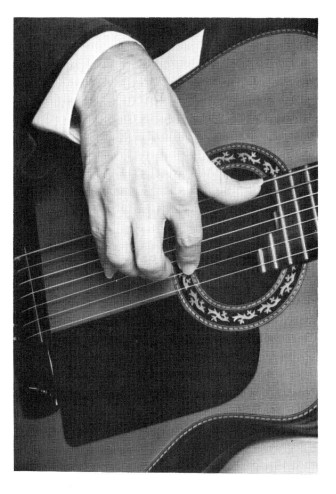

*Rest stroke:* position of index finger as it strikes the first string, having just moved through the space in front of the first string

Position of index finger *after* striking first string and having *followed through* by coming to rest on the second string

## Alternating index and middle fingers

For speed and fluency, practice playing the index and middle fingers one after the other. Other standard rest stroke combinations are *m-a, i-a, i-m-a* and their reverse orders. Practice them, too.

Do take the time to develop a good rest stroke, especially if you are using a nylon string guitar. Otherwise, the melody of the solo arrangement will recede into the accompanying notes and what you are playing will sound like backup fingerpicking.

## Left hand position

If sometimes you've wrapped your left hand thumb around the guitar neck for the occasional odd chord, or to bend notes, fine. *But,* if you've been parking it there all the time, the moment to stop resisting and start putting it where it belongs is—at-hand. For the complexities of fingerstyle guitar it is imperative to put the left hand thumb well under the neck and centered between the two middle fingers. Do it now while you still have easier material to work on! If you have difficulty remembering this position, tape a drinking straw down the middle of your guitar neck as a mechanical thumb barrier. After a week or two you will have a trained thumb. Or a flattened straw.

**Ok, now, play it again, Sam, and this time stick your fingers into it**
Using index and middle fingers, alternately, and with rest strokes, play the solo
again. Complex, constantly changing right hand fingering will be carefully notated
in this book. But here there is only one rule: use alternate *i-m* with rest strokes. If
you forget what finger you are supposed to be on in your alternation, continue with
either one. In the big picture, it doesn't matter.

**A message to the worried**
If you think you played *Pick a Simple Tune* with great control and good jazz
phrasing, then—well, I'm tempted to say that you are probably deceiving yourself!
As basic as this technique is, it is one of the hardest to master for someone
accustomed to using a flat pick. Some switch-over (pick-to-fingers) jazz guitarists
*never* get this *i-m* alternation smoothly, and instead play linear material with a
(palmed) flat pick, or with other fingers or give up on linear material! I'll mention
some other techniques  later, as they are, in my opinion, of secondary importance
to the primary *i-m* technique.

*Watch* and *listen* to fingerstyle jazz, classical and flamenco guitarists play linear
material—bass players, too.

**Stay with it—**

I really *do* mean to belabor the importance of developing the *i-m* rest stroke technique and to encourage you to stay at it. I *know* that it is hard, slow, and clumsy at this point. I recall clearly when I switched over. At that stage of my life I had been studying pick style jazz guitar with Jimmy Raney and Jim Hall. Replete with ego, I started studying fingerstyle technique with classical guitarist Albert Valdes-Blain. It was a most humbling experience. It was frustrating beyond tolerance, and daily I wanted to throw myself, my guitar, or Mr. Valdes-Blain out the window. I have absolute compassion for you. If we all lived in the same city I would set up a crisis intervention phone counseling service for flat pickers switching to *i-m* rest stroke. Treat yourself kindly, and stay with it.

Also, start letting your right hand fingernails grow, as they are very valuable for tone production. More on this later. If you are the nervous type, bite your left hand nails only.

**Further exercises and supplementary material**

Practice your *i-m* technique with already familiar linear material, such as scales, favorite licks, jazz melodies, transcribed solos, etc. Classical material for single note instruments is valuable, too. I especially like the Bach unaccompanied violin and cello material, such as the *Partitas and Sonatas for Violin*, because of their similarity to jazz. Eighth note flow and harmonic movement are well illustrated.

Since fingerstyle jazz technique is essentially classical guitar technique, I recommend your using a good classical guitar method for supplementary exercises. One book is *The Complete Method for Classical Guitar* (Mel Bay, Pub.), another, *The Complete Carcassi Guitar Method* (Mel Bay, Pub.).

**Tips**
**About teachers**

While it is possible to use this book by yourself, I encourage you to find a teacher for fingerstyle jazz. Unfortunately, the availability of qualified teachers of a "new" and complex guitar form is always a few years behind the popularization of the form. If you cannot find a fingerstyle jazz teacher, seek out a classical guitar teacher to help you with your technique and put together your own program with the aid of this book and any other appropriate material. This is the route I went, some fifteen years ago, when even in New York I couldn't find a fingerstyle jazz teacher. If you are a fingerstyle player who plays no jazz, then a traditional pick-style jazz teacher can help you with the *feeling* of jazz.

| | |
|---|---|
| **Etude Two:** | *Still Evening, Silent Stars* |
| **Concept:** | Arpeggiating chords as an approach to soloing |
| **Technique:** | Right hand: a) flat pick: normal technique |
| | b) fingerstyle: arpeggiation fingering and the free stroke |
| | Left hand: holding fingers in chord form positions |

The use of constant arpeggiation is another way of keeping the rhythm and harmony going in solo guitar playing.

*Still Evening, Silent Stars* is a vehicle to illustrate the use of arpeggios and arpeggio fingering for both right and left hand.

### Two kinds of arpeggios
In pick jazz guitar playing, arpeggios are often *articulated*. The notes are played one at a time, detached, most often in the context of movable position-oriented scales. In fingerstyle playing this is done, too, but there is also much use of arpeggios whose notes are *sustained*. These are often fingered from chord forms, rather than scale positions, with horizontal/vertical, open position/movable position approaches mixed freely. You will see the blend when you play this etude.

### Playing arpeggios fingerstyle with the left hand
To make the notes of an arpeggio ring together, keep the left hand fingers in place. Stay on the "tip-toes of your fingertips" so that the fingers won't block adjacent strings from ringing.

### The free stroke and arpeggiation fingering of the right hand
In Etude One, the *linear work* was typically played with the *i-m* combination *traveling across the strings*, with no regard to what finger was on which string. A rest stroke was used for emphasis.

The *free stroke is used primarily where several strings must be kept ringing*. In sustained arpeggio work a series of rest strokes would damp still-ringing lower adjacent strings. Since a free stroke is usually played with a lighter touch, it can be used to play *unaccented* notes. Chords are also played with free strokes (chord technique will be discussed later). Begin in the same position as the rest stroke. Using the *i* finger, strike the first string by brushing or flicking it with the left side of the fingertip and nail. *Let the finger follow through toward the palm of the hand without coming to rest on the adjacent strings.* As with the rest stroke, there should be some flex in the first tip segment. Do not freeze the fingers in a rigid hooked position and pull directly upward, as it will result in a "splang" effect made by the string slapping against the fret board. Also, make sure that only the fingers are moving and don't let the hand bounce upward. Think of the rest of your hand as a platform from which your fingers are operating.

*Free stroke:* position of index finger as it strikes the first string, having just moved through the space in front of the first string

Position of index finger *after* striking first string and having followed through by clearing the adjacent lower strings

## The thumb

The thumb most often executes a free stroke. except during the few times when the bass notes form a melody which needs to be emphasized. To begin, temporarily rest the first three fingers on the first string. Then, move thumb in a forward circular movement, clipping the sixth string with the lower, outer edge of the thumb tip and nail. When making a free stroke, this action will clear the adjacent string. If your thumb is naturally curved outward and back, you can execute this stroke without bending the first tip segment forward. If you have a straight thumb, you may want to bend the first tip segment a little.

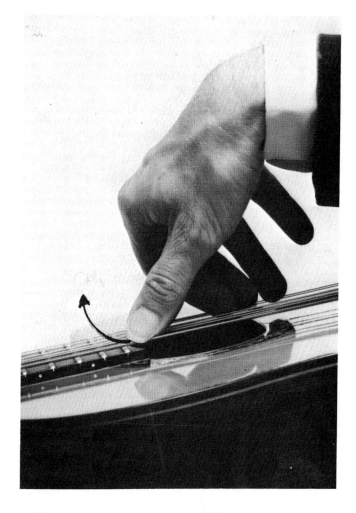

*Free stroke:* position of thumb as it strikes the lowest string, having just moved through the space in front of the string, and about to clear the next lowest string

Position of thumb having just cleared the string next to the lowest string, and about to return through an elliptical orbit to its beginning position

### Pre-setting right hand fingers

In *fingerstyle arpeggio work*, as in Etude Two, the notes of an arpeggio lie sequentially across several strings. The thumb (*p*) can play the lowest strings, and the *i, m* and *a* fingers can play one note apiece for each of the following higher strings.

When both *notes* and *strings* occur in a repeated pattern, the right hand *fingers* may be pre-set to the same pattern so that the same notes and strings are played by the same fingers.

When pre-setting fingers, make sure the fingers merely *hover* over the strings, and *do not rest directly* on the strings. If you come to rest on the strings before repeating each pattern, you will cancel out the previously ringing strings.

## Arpeggio warm-ups for the right hand

Here are some exercises for you to get used to a variety of right hand arpeggio patterns. These are to be done on open strings, so that you can pay attention to your right hand. Notice how the fingers of the hand often stay in the same configuration.

Directions: Use a free stroke. Right hand fingering is above, string number is below.

Code

| p | thumb |
|---|---|
| i | index finger |
| m | middle finger |
| a | ring finger |

1.  p  i  m     p  i  m     p  i  m     fingers
    3  2  1     3  2  1     3  2  1     strings

2.  p  i  m     p  i  m     p  i  m     p  i  m
    6  5  4     5  4  3     4  3  2     3  2  1

3.  p  i  m     p  i  m     p  i  m     p  i  m
    6  2  1     5  2  1     4  2  1     3  2  1

4.  p  m  i     p  m  i     p  m  i     p  m  i
    6  1  2     5  1  2     4  1  2     3  1  2

5.  m  i  p     m  i  p     m  i  p     m  i  p
    4  5  6     3  4  5     2  3  4     1  2  3

6.  p  i  a     p  i  a     p  i  a     p  i  a
    5  3  1     6  4  2     5  3  1     6  4  2

7.  p  i  a     p  i  m     p  i  a     p  i  m
    5  3  1     4  3  2     5  3  1     4  3  2

8.  p  i  m     a  m  i     p  i  m     a  m  i
    5  3  2     1  2  3     6  5  4     3  2  1

9.  p  i  m  a     p  i  m  a     p  i  m  a
    4  3  2  1     5  3  2  1     6  3  2  1

10. p  i  m  a     p  i  m  a     p  i  m  a
    6  5  4  3     5  4  3  2     4  3  2  1

11. p  p  i  m  a     p  p  i  m  a*
    6  5  4  3  2     5  4  3  2  1

12. p  p  p  i  m  a     p  p  p  i  m  a
    6  5  4  3  2  1     6  5  4  3  2  1

*Note: when the thumb plucks two or three notes in a row in the same direction, use a very light rest stroke and push through to each string, rather than making a complete elliptical follow-through after each pluck.

**Arpeggio patterns for *Still Evening, Silent Stars***

It would be unrealistic for me to write a jazz piece with only one arpeggio pattern, because jazz just doesn't sound that way. So here is a more typical situation in *Still Evening, Silent Stars*, an exercise inspired by *Corcovado* (Antonio Carlos Jobim).

There are eight right hand patterns which vary only slightly from each other. Here they are written with open strings so that you can practice them before adding the fingered notes. The number of each fingering pattern illustration corresponds to the same pattern in the piece. In this piece, the corresponding measures are identified by the same illustration number, e.g. ☐1 .

⌣() indicates a tie or slur, neither of which requires a right hand fingering

| 1 | a | p | p | i | m | a | m | i |
|---|---|---|---|---|---|---|---|---|
|   | 2 | 6 | 5 | 4 | 3 | 2 | 3 | 4 |

| 2 | a | p | p | i | m | a ⌣() | m |
|---|---|---|---|---|---|---|---|
|   | 1 | 5 | 4 | 3 | 2 | 2 | 3 |

| 3 | a | p | p | p | m | i | m | a |
|---|---|---|---|---|---|---|---|---|
|   | 2 | 6 | 5 | 4 | 2 | 3 | 2 | 1 |

| 4 | m | i | m ⌣() | i | p | p | i |
|---|---|---|---|---|---|---|---|
|   | 1 | 2 | 3 | 3 | 5 | 4 | 3 |

| 5 | m | p | p | p | i | m | i | m |
|---|---|---|---|---|---|---|---|---|
|   | 3 | 6 | 5 | 4 | 3 | 2 | 3 | 2 |

| 6 | a | p | p | p | i | m | a | m |
|---|---|---|---|---|---|---|---|---|
|   | 1 | 6 | 5 | 4 | 3 | 2 | ] | 2 |

| 7 | a | p | p ⌣() | i | m | a | m |
|---|---|---|---|---|---|---|---|
|   | 1 | 5 | 4 | 3 | 2 | 1 | 2 |

| 8 | a | p | p | i ⌣() | m | a | m |
|---|---|---|---|---|---|---|---|
|   | 1 | 5 | 4 | 3 | 2 | 1 | 2 |

| 9 | a | p | i | m | a ⌣()⌣() | m |
|---|---|---|---|---|---|---|
|   | 2 | 5 | 4 | 3 | 2 | 3 |

**Barring**

Many measures in *Still Evening, Silent Stars* contain chords which require a five or six string barre with the index finger. So that the adjacent strings will not be blocked and can ring into each other, you *must* play on the very tips of the other needed fingers. In some cases, in order to do this, you may want to barre further across the neck than just the strings you absolutely need to make the other fingers become more perpendicular to the fretboard. On the other hand, don't barre further than is necessary for clear sounds.

*Similie* written above or below a measure means that the right hand fingering pattern and/or left hand string sequence is the same as in the previous measure.

# Still Evening, Silent Stars

Adm

Concert with the American Brass Quintet,
Aspen Music Festival, 1971

Photo by Arabella Simon

**Further exercises**

Arpeggio work is used a lot for folk and country music soloing and accompaniment. One good book on the subject is *The Anthology of Fingerstyle Guitar*, by Tommy Flint (Mel Bay, Pub.).

Also, almost any classical guitar method book has sections on arpeggiation. Composers of the early nineteenth century, such as Carulli, Carcassi, Giuliani and Aquado wrote many exercises and pieces using arpeggiation. Examples: *The Best of Giuliani* and *The Best of Carulli* by Joseph Castle (Mel Bay, Pub.).

**Tips**

**Cramped neck?**

When you are holding your left hand fingers down for sustained arpeggios near the nut of your guitar, are you cramped for room? Do your fingers accidentally damp neighboring strings which are supposed to be ringing? Extra narrow guitar necks are a problem for fingerstyle players, especially if the players have broad fingers. This is why classical guitars always have wider necks. If you are having a problem with cramped quarters near the nut, an experienced repair man might be able to remedy the situation.

If your guitar neck has a binding (the wider the better), then more than likely the frets reach only *to* it, and not *through* it right to the edges. Have the repair man pull out the first few frets and put in new ones which go through the binding right *to* the edges of the neck. Tell him not to make a long taper at the edge of the fret, but just a rounding of the ends. This will allow for extra space, over-all 1/16″ to 1/8″.

Another way to achieve this wider spacing is to take certain wider neck twelve string guitars (such as some Martins and Guilds) and have the bridge, saddle and nut replaced and/or regrooved for six strings.

| | |
|---|---|
| Etude Three: | *Huggable You* |
| Concept: | Sustaining bass note used as accompanying device with linear or arpeggiated melody immediately following |
| Technique: | Right hand: a) flat pick: normal technique<br>b) fingerstyle: arpeggiation fingering mixed with linear fingering |
| | Left hand: holding bass notes in place while moving others |

## Fingerstyle for two handed lap piano

To the casually observing pick player, the difference between pick and fingerstyle solo jazz guitar appears to be the right hand. And that is true—at the beginning stages only. That is, if you learn a minimum of fingerstyle technique, with no other changes, you *can* play a sort of solo jazz guitar. Conceptually, it would be a pick-oriented style which you happen to be playing with your fingers. A lot of players do this, and produce fine jazz. Even so, what they are missing is the opportunity to play "two handed piano" on the guitar, an aspect which I feel is the true cachet of unaccompanied solo guitar. The specifics of this aspect are explained in detail as the book progresses, and starting in Part Two, the etudes will be played with fingers only.

## Music in two parts

In most jazz piano playing, the lower end of the piano keyboard is played with the left hand, which, in a simple sense, can be considered to be the accompanying hand to the right. One basic accompanying device is the sustained bass note, played as a separate part as the lead line is played. For now, the bass note will always precede the lead, which follows immediately.

Examine a few measures of *Huggable You*:

| Conceptually, think: | lower part | upper part |
|---|---|---|
| | bass sustains | melody moves |
| | note stems point down | note stems point up |
| | thumb plays bass note | fingers play melody |
| | or, in piano terms: | |
| | bass clef: left hand | treble clef: right hand |

Both upper and lower parts have separate rhythms, with the upper part generally moving faster than the bass part. This is because, at least in this instance, the bass notes move at the pace of the chord progression, which most often moves only once or twice per measure. The first measure of this example is an exception.

Notice how the direction of the stems of notes are used to separate notes of the same time value. In this example, they separate eighth notes from half and quarter notes.

## Linear material and arpeggiation mixed

*Huggable You* can be thought of as a combination of the two previous Etudes, since it contains both linear material, as in Etude One, and sustained arpeggiation, as in Etude Two. The new addition is the sustained bass note followed by linear material. To warm up for this situation, practice anchoring low notes (chord tones) and playing scalar ideas while the note is still ringing. It will become immediately apparent that the finger holding down the low note will not be available for the single line above. It *will* take some getting used to!

Try this sample and then make up some of your own. The first C is to be played free stroke. Why?

## Fingering

For the moment ignore the right hand fingering since it isn't needed for the first *pick* run-through. But follow the left hand absolutely! There are other fingering possibilities, but they aren't the ones you would come up with at this point, I suspect. The tendency is to retreat to simpler fingering, avoiding the newer left hand fingerstyle orientation.

Use your pick to play *Huggable You*, which is an improvisation on the chord changes of *Embraceable You* (George and Ira Gershwin), using the two part concept described above.

## Once more, digitally

How did it go? Next, play *Huggable You* fingerstyle. Pay *very* strict attention to the right hand fingering *now*. Note that when the improvisation shifts from arpeggios to linear sections the right hand fingering correspondingly shifts to *i-m*. The *a* finger is often used in bridging sections, or when the phrase is part linear and part arpeggio work.

# Huggable You

## Supplementary material
The sit-on-a-note-while-playing-other notes style is explored in George Van Eps'
*Harmonic Mechanisms, Vols. I, II, and III* (Mel Bay, Pub.). They are amazing books,
and I recommend them wholeheartedly.

## Tips
## Making guitars feel the same
Do you have guitar switching problems? If you can jump from playing
a Telecaster with super slinky strings to a Dreadnought with ski chair
cables for strings, or perhaps a nylon classical with a wide neck and
high action, stop here. You don't need to know this. God blessed you.
I'm envious.

But, if you are merely mortal, like me, you probably would like your
guitars to feel as similar to each other as possible. Here are some hints
on how to do it.

*Neck widths and scale lengths* are two factors. If you are buying your
first solid body, nylon, and acoustic steel guitars all at once, you can
choose fairly similar *scale lengths*. Just take a yardstick along and
measure from the nut to the same fret on all three instruments. *Neck
width* is harder. For fingerstyle playing wider necks are better, so
instruments such as Les Pauls, D-35's and almost any nylon-string
guitar are better than narrower-necked similar category instruments.
The problem is that wider necks *and* same scale lengths don't always
belong to the same guitar.

*Body sizes and shapes* are another factor. Classical guitars are
uniformly the same. Steel string flat tops are basically Dreadnaught
size or smaller. The smaller steels will be closer to the nylon instrument. In the solid body instruments, none are as thick as nylon and
steel string instruments. Being a sit-down guitarist, I like a solid body
guitar that won't disappear in my lap, which basically means one
with a wider upper bout. Jazz guitar body choices are easier because
there is more variety than in the other styles. If your Tele is your main
instrument, a Super 400 is probably not the one for you.*

It won't be easy, working with stock models only, to come up with a
nylon, steel acoustic, and electric that have the same width necks,
same scale lengths, and similar body sizes. It's especially true in
today's marketplace, where most solid bodies, for instance, come in
only about four shapes—Les Paul, Tele, Strat, SG. Check used vintage
models, small manufacturers, outdated, once popular guitars, and
don't be a snob about names and models—go for odd-ball guitars that
feel and sound right, no matter what the brand name, if similarity is
the name of the game.

Finally, there is the custom-built route, the most expensive and the
best chance for having instruments similar to each other. Over the
years and out of necessity, I went this route. When I caught seven-
string fever from George Van Eps, my six-string guitars were even-
tually sold, traded, or rebuilt into seven-strings with identical-feeling
necks and similar body shapes.

*I mention instrument brand and model names for size similarities or dissimilarities only and not as
specific endorsements.

| | |
|---|---|
| **Etude Four:** | *Nectarine* |
| **Concept:** | Alternating chordal comping as filler with single line phrases |
| **Technique:** | Right hand: a) flat pick: chord comping and single note picking<br>b) fingerstyle: linear playing with *i-m*, and *a*, with some arpeggiation; chord plucking with *p-i-m-a* |
| | Left hand: normal (pick style) chordal and linear fingering |

### Self accompanying by comping

Since all of us jazz pick players grew up learning how to play both lead and rhythm guitar, it's not surprising to find pick players now punctuating their own single note solos with rhythmic chord fillers. Actually, this way of playing, as common as it is today, is not really *so* old—Django Rheinhardt and Charlie Christian, for instance, did not play that way, and neither do *all* of today's players. Jim Hall is a master of it, as is Joe Pass in his unaccompanied solo playing.

### How to do it

This kind of chordal comping is used to fill the gaps between phrases of single line playing, so *leave room for it!* If you anxiously run-on phrases, you won't ever have an opportunity to use this style. Think of vocal songs with your phrases corresponding to the words. The spaces *between sentences (and phrases)* are the spots to play chords. This is shown in the comping style of *Nectarine*, following. *Think ahead* in your single line phrasing, so that you can see where and when the chord punctuation will be coming up. Any familiar chord forms will work if done with taste.

*Nectarine* is playable both pick style and fingerstyle.

### Pick style

For pick style there is no special problem, so just go to it.

### Fingerstyle: further use of the *a* finger

In this Etude the *a* finger is used in places where standard *i-m* might be possible, but awkward. In instances such as the first phrase of the piece, there is a one-finger-per-string situation which can be played *a-m-i*, in an arpeggiation pattern, played rest stroke:

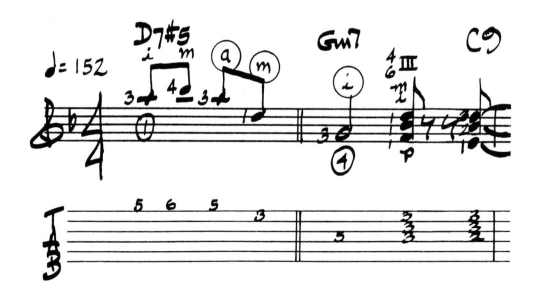

The use of *a* on the A note *sets up* the easier movement of the following *m* and especially the *i* which needs to skip a string. In fingering one of your arrangements you can see what is coming next, and can make accommodations such as this. In improvisation you don't always have the advantage of foresight.

Generally, then, the *a* finger can be used as it is in this piece for:
   a) setting up smooth string-to-string movements of *i-m*, as in measures one, two and six
   b) making leaps up and over several strings, especially after *i-m* have descended to the lower strings, as in measure seven
   c) four note and sometimes three note chords, as in measures nine and seventeen.

Take a look at Etude One and see if it would be advantageous in certain instances to use the *a* finger.

## Chord plucking
For *fingerstyle*, the single line playing is primarily *i-m rest stroke* with occasional *a* fingerings. For the chords, use the arpeggiation approach of one-finger-per-string. Four note chords demand that *p-i-m-a* are used, and three usually need *p-i-m*. My guess is that even if you, as a pick player, have not played extensive fingerstyle before now, you probably have plucked chords from time to time.

Check your right hand technique and make sure that:
   a) your thumb is out to the left with fingers close together. No eagle's claw!
   b) you are *plucking* individual strings and not merely brushing them.
   c) immediately after plucking the chord, your fingers are curling under in their follow through, in *free-stroke* fashion. Don't freeze your hand in one hooking position and pluck by yanking the whole thing up and out!

## Going for it
If you intend on going for good right hand technique and haven't begun your major effort, now's the time to dig in and get to work. I know that when I first started *thinking* fingerstyle arrangements my right hand technique lagged behind and couldn't execute my ideas.

Here is *Nectarine*, then, a good old-timey swing chorus on the chord changes of *Tangerine* (Johnny Mercer and Victor Scherzinger).

## Further exercises and supplementary material
Single note melody lines plus chord fills, and chord-melody style plus single line fills (see Etude Five) have existed for a long while within flat pick playing styles. Look for unaccompanied solo material for pick guitar to see what you can glean for solo jazz guitar, pick and fingerstyle. Here are three books with a variety of styles that all display alternating chord and line playing: *Tony Mottola Guitar Styles* by Tony Mottola (Mel Bay, Pub.), *The Liturgical Guitarist* by Bill Bay (Mel Bay, Pub.), and *The Guitar Virtuoso* by Harry Volpe (Mel Bay, Pub.).

# Nectarine

33

**Tips**

**The importance of carefully choosing an accompaniment**

I think of accompanying a melody in the same way a chef once told me about cooking a dinner. "Since the raw material is already perfect at the start," he said, "if you want to ruin it by cooking and saucing, you must do it *very* carefully."

| Etude Five: | *How's By You?* |
|---|---|
| Concept: | Chord melody playing with single note fills |
| Technique: | Right hand: a) flat pick: chords and linear playing |
| |                  b) fingerstyle: chords and linear playing |
| | Left hand:   normal (pick style) chordal and linear fingering |

## Using our history

If you were to look through music periodicals from the nineteen twenties and thirties, you would see, in the plectrum banjo articles, discussions of chord-melody style. As guitarists, that's our inheritance. Four note block chords and their inversions are the *total* stylistic repertoire of what most pick players use to play solo guitar. For them, "solo guitar" *equals* block-chord melody solos.

## Then and now

And why not? It works, especially when used with a rhythm section accompaniment. However, as an unaccompanied solo style . . . On plectrum banjo, to keep the rhythmic feel going during half notes, whole notes, and rests, the banjoist just kept strumming away at the same chord—a la Eddie Peabody in *The World Is Waiting For The Sunrise.* That style doesn't exist in today's guitar playing, so for unaccompanied solo guitar playing, *single note fills* can keep the rhythm going, giving contrast and excitement.

This style is of course closely related to the style used in the previous Etude, *Nectarine.* Here in *How's By You?* the *melody* is in chords, the *fills* are single notes. In *Nectarine* the reverse was true. Traditionally, as in *How's By You?*, when the melody is slower moving and in chord melody format, the single note fills have faster note values. When the single note melody has faster note values as in *Nectarine*, the chord comping has slower note values. Where and when the change from chords to lines takes place is exactly the same in both styles: between phrases.

There is no special *pick style* technique needed for *How's By You?*, based on the harmony of *What's New?* (Johnny Burke and Bob Haggart). The *fingerstyle* technique for this piece requires one new component: playing a four note chord (*p, i, m, a*) immediately followed by one or more single notes. Since all the right hand fingers will be used in plucking the chord you will have to repeat a finger for the note following:

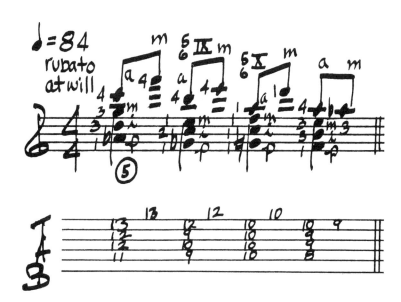

Theoretically you could use the *e* finger, but unless you have much fingerstyle experience, hold off on it for a while.

If there is more than one single note following, alternation can then be employed:

Now that you have been working with fingerstyle technique for a while, I am leaving the more obvious fingering situations for you to figure out.

Practice this style with any pieces you already play. It works most easily in a rubato or slow tempo, but can certainly be played as up tempo as your chops and mind allow. Listen to what great jazz improvisers filled in behind singers of any period of jazz. You couldn't go wrong by studying what was played behind Billie Holiday, for instance. Also see Etude Four,(p.32).

**Technical note**
Make sure in your chord plucking to emphasize the top note, since it is the improvised melody note.

**Tips**
**Getting stuck between strings?**
In your early stages of working with *i-m*, rest stroke, it is common to have your fingers get stuck or trip up between strings. This usually comes from *dipping downward* toward the face of the guitar during the rest stroke, when the fingers should be *pulling across* from string to string.

One way of becoming aware of your fingers dipping downward is to purposely pluck over the pickup (or fretboard) and listen and feel for fingernail clicks on top of the pickup cover. You'll know right away. Stay there until you click no more.

Getting stuck happens more easily on a steel stringed instrument than on a nylon. When I play on steel strings, I use an even more shallow attack, picking nail-to-nail from string-to-string. Speaking of nails, don't grow them so long that *they* will trip you up.

In short: Pull, don't dip.

# How's By You?

38

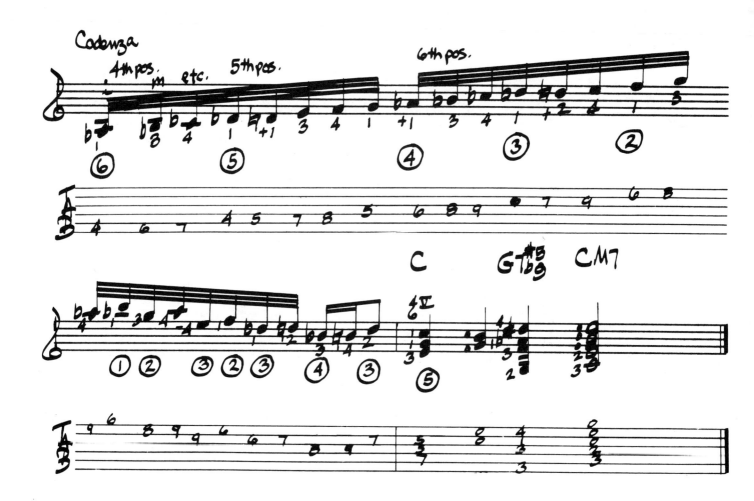

Aspen, Colorado, 1971

Photo by Joan Klyhn

| | |
|---|---|
| Etude Six: | *Less, Being More* |
| Concept: | Using thirds, fourths, and fifths as chord partials in self-accompaniment |
| Technique: | Right hand: a) flat pick: picking two notes on adjacent strings with upper line moving as melody note and lower sustaining as accompaniment<br>b) fingerstyle: plucking two note groups on adjacent strings followed by upper single line in various combinations of *p, i, m, a*<br>Left hand: Moving upper melody notes while sustaining lower accompanying notes |

I'd like to mention here that, in order to keep this book manageable, the position I have taken is that melody (lead line—improvisation) is paramount. The main task at hand is to create a single line that can stand alone, or, if it does not, to provide some sort of simple accompaniment to it. Not all aspects of arranging are covered—counterpoint, for instance, or voice leading beyond simple considerations.

## One note accompaniment
If you grew up fascinated by the harmonic aspect of the guitar, as I did, then somewhere along the way you probably struggled to play a piano arrangement on the guitar. And couldn't. You discovered that there weren't enough strings and fingers to match note-for-note what a pianist could play. And isn't more notes at once always better than less?

Not necessarily. With careful choices, fewer notes can imply more. When I found that out I could finally let go of the more-is-better idea.

Further: if a single note melody alone can demonstrate the harmonic progression of a piece, as shown in Etude One, then to have even one other note played *at the same time* is a bonanza of harmonic riches. And—the melody must still do *its* work to show the harmonic movement of a piece.

## The language of intervals
Before beginning the single note accompanying of a melody, be sure to review the names and places of the various intervals contained in major, minor, and dominant seventh chords.

## Major triad

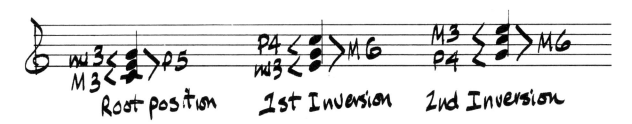

## Minor triad

## Dominant seventh

Root position    1st Inversion    2nd Inversion    3rd Inversion

### Implying a major triad with a major third

Each measure below begins with a *major third*. The lower sustained note is the root of the major chord indicated, and the first melody note above it is a major third higher.* The notes following are part of the major scale from which the chord comes. They all contain the perfect fifth of the chord. The other notes may imply a major sixth or major seventh chord, but the core tonality is clear: *major*.

### Implying a minor triad with a minor third

The root of each minor chord below accompanies the melody above, the first note of which is always a *minor third* above. Most measures contain a perfect fifth in the melody, with the exception of two. Because the two are in the context of a series of minor chords, your ear will hear them also as complete minor chords.

*When playing two notes simultaneously on adjacent strings, notes on the higher string can not be played rest stroke without damping the lower string. Instead, use a forceful free stroke.

## Implying a dominant seventh chord with a minor third

In the illustration below, the first melody note of each measure happens to be the fifth of the chord indicated above.* Placing a *major* third below it would result in implying a totally different chord, so a minor third is the appropriate interval of the major triad contained in the dominant seventh chord. By itself, the minor third created by C and E♭ *could* imply a C minor chord, but with the addition of the following A♭ and G♭, the root and minor seventh of the A♭ dominant seventh chord, there is no doubt about the function of the minor third on the first beat. The A♭ alone is all that is needed to complete the major triad, and, of course, the G♭ is essential to turn the chord into a dominant seventh.

*For simplicity and clarity, the intervals being demonstrated are the first ones in every measure. In actual playing this will not be the case. If the first note is an upper or lower neighbor, as long as the next note is the needed third, fine. Also, you don't *have* to put the accompanying note on the first beat.

## Perfect fourths and fifths

If Gregorian chants or Hollywood's version of oriental music appeals to you, you will like successive parallel fourths or fifths only. However, since neither can be used alone to identify a major or minor tonality, they should be used in conjunction with other harmonies which do. Include the third of the triad, for example. Below is an example of accompanying with perfect fifths. Check for thirds.

## Augmented fourths/diminished fifths

Augmented fourths, or diminished fifths, are a different story, as they are a most efficient harmonic sound. Alone they make up the third and seventh (or vice versa depending on above/below placement) of a dominant seventh chord. Here is a partial cycle of fifths pattern of dominant sevenths. Notice that *both* the root and fifth of any one chord need not be used to achieve a complete dominant seventh sound.

Augmented fourths and diminished fifths are used a lot in blues, so I have written Etude Six, *Less, Being More...* as an illustration of this.

44

# Less, Being More...

Adm

## Larger Intervals

To play larger intervals with a pick, it is necessary to skip across damped strings, in quick arpeggio fashion. And beyond a one string skip, it is really awkward, nearly impossible. On the other hand, the forte of fingerstyle guitar *is* playing large intervals simultaneously on non-adjacent strings. Therefore, I have restricted intervals played with a pick to only those on two adjacent strings. I do realize this is a somewhat artificial cutoff point, and it is for a purpose.

## Sixths

The reach of the average hand is about that of a sixth on adjacent strings. Though it is possible to use sixths played in this manner, they are somewhat awkward:

Sixths are more easily played fingerstyle, in the skipped string manner, and are taken up again in chapter twelve.

## Further exercises and supplementary material

Take existing single note material (tunes, transcribed solos, your own improvisations, etc.) and practice accompanying them with single notes making up (at crucial spots) thirds, fourths, and fifths. Start simply with whole notes and half notes as the bottom part.

### Tips
### If in doubt, leave it out

In most orchestral arranging, choices must be made in regard to what notes of a chord are going to be duplicated. In guitar arranging, it's easy: it's not necessary to duplicate. The chord tones of the *line* represent their place in the harmony. You don't need to play the same ones in the accompaniment. If it happens, fine, but it's not necessary.

| | |
|---|---|
| **Etude Seven:** | *Even More Less* |
| **Concept:** | Two note accompaniment to a single line, using thirds, fourths, fifths, and sixths as chord partials |
| **Technique:** | Right hand:  a) flat pick: picking three notes on adjacent strings with upper melody line moving and two accompanying lower notes sustaining |
| | b) fingerstyle: plucking three note groups on adjacent strings, with upper melody line moving and two accompanying lower notes sustaining. Various combinations of *p, i, m, a* |
| | Left hand:  Moving upper melody notes while sustaining lower accompanying notes. |

## More melodic freedom

Two note accompaniments of thirds, fourths, fifths, and sixths allow for more use of upper chord partials in the melody. Just remember that the more non-chord tones are in the melody the more necessary it is for the accompaniment to imply the basic triad.

## Thirds as accompaniments to upper moving line

Examine how the accompanying major and minor thirds plus the melody imply the sound of ninth chords in this harmonized major scale:

Notice that in two note accompaniment two fingers are committed to play a certain rhythm, time and location, and thus are momentarily not available as melody players.

## Augmented fourths/diminished fifths as accompaniments to upper moving line

Augmented fourths and diminished fifths as accompaniment can also imply extended dominant seventh sounds, such as the dominant ninth and thirteenth chords in this pattern:

Here is a variation of the above with the melody moved up an octave.

But this next version has to be played fingerstyle because the top note lies too many strings away for comfortable pick playing of the first chord.

## Sixths as accompaniment to upper moving line

Here is a sample of how sixths can be used to accompany a melody. These are adjacent string sixths with an adjacent string melody, which usually results in very stretchy situations for the left hand. Skipped string sixths are taken up in the fingerstyle-only part two of this book and are easier to play.

## All together, now

Etude Eight, *Even More Less* is a mix of one and two note accompaniments making up thirds, fourths, fifths, and sixths. When there is more choice of accompaniment devices, more attention can be paid to how each individual note moves in the accompaniment. Smaller movements are generally preferred over larger.

## Further exercises and supplementary material

Take whatever scales you practice and harmonize them in thirds, fourths, fifths and sixths, so that you can produce them at will for accompanying. A master of minimal playing that implies more is Jimmy Wyble, and his book, *The Art of Two-Line Improvisation* (Flat Five, Pub.),* is full of ingenious studies. I cannot recommend it highly enough.


*Exclusive Distributor—Mel Bay Publications

# Even More Less

| Etude Eight: | *Starboy* |
|---|---|
| Concept: | Reviewing all concepts presented so far |
| Technique: | Right and left hand, flat pick and fingerstyle: reviewing all techniques to date. |

*Starboy* uses all of the concepts presented to date: single lines unaccompanied, arpeggios, some with sustained bass notes, alternating single lines and chordal comping, chord melody with single line fills, and chord partials as accompaniment devices. All of these concepts can be utilized with a pick *or* fingerstyle.

For all of those concepts and the accompanying techniques, the piece doesn't look over-stuffed, or chock full cellar to ceiling. This shows that solo guitar music need not be a case of more being better. You don't have to be a one-man band to play solo guitar, you just need to play solo guitar. And solo guitar, at core, has to do with playing music which is *complete in content,* not how extensive a repertoire of tricks and devices you have. The concepts and techniques in this book will clothe your basic ideas, but you need to have something of content to begin with.

*Starboy* is based on the harmony of *Sunny* (Bobby Hebb).

## Supplementary material
You now have enough of an idea of some of what goes into making up solo jazz guitar to make sense of different players' approaches. Listen to the records of: Joe Pass, Lenny Breau, Luiz Bonfa, Ted Greene, Laurindo Almeida, Charlie Byrd, Ralph Towner, Baden Powell, Earl Klugh, George Van Eps, and Bucky Pizzarelli. See what printed arrangements you can find by these artists. Joe Pass is such a current figurehead that you might enjoy the transcriptions of his unaccompanied solos in *Joe Pass Chord Solos,* by Joe Pass (Gwyn Publishing Co., Pub.).

**Tips**
**The convenience of intimacy**
Because of the nature of solo guitar and the volume at which it is played I've never needed any more equipment than I can carry in my hands and on my shoulder. With my acoustics, my amp is a Princeton Reverb head, attached to a small, sealed, ported stereo enclosure with a ten inch speaker. If I use my 7-string electric I bring a slightly larger similar enclosure instead. In a situation requiring more volume I jack into the club or auditorium house system, or have my amp miked. Never do I crank my amplifier up all the way, taking a chance that my acoustic instruments will howl, scream or whistle. That's what my audience will do, I hope.

# Starboy

*on the optional cassette recording, this break is the beginning of Etude 18.

# PART TWO: CONCEPTS AND TECHNIQUES UNIQUE TO FINGERSTYLE GUITAR

| | |
|---|---|
| **Etude Nine:** | *The Persistence of Gershwin* |
| **Concept:** | Accompanying melodic lines with simultaneously played bass notes lying two or more strings away |
| **Technique:** | Fingerstyle only |
| | Right hand: *i, m,* and *a,* rest stroke, play melody, *p,* free stroke, plays bass |
| | Left hand: more complex fingering and stretching to accommodate bigger intervals between melody and bass |

## Fingerstyle-only solo jazz guitar
Using pick only, you can play a whole lot of unaccompanied solo jazz guitar. To play exactly the same thing with your fingers is pointless. It's hardly worth all of the effort involved in learning decent fingerstyle right hand technique just to be able to say "Look ma! No pick!" Ma wouldn't even notice the difference, unless she is another guitarist who can discern the technicalities. So just flailing your phalanges isn't the point.

## The point
Now that you have come this far on this trip you have a context in which to understand the following: *The single most important distinguishing feature of fingerstyle-only solo jazz guitar is the use of two or more simultaneously played notes lying on non-adjacent strings.*

## Once more, from near the top
The technique of accompanying a melody with a preceding "piano left hand" lower accompanying note was introduced in Etude Three, *Huggable You.* With fingerstyle technique, you can also play these bass notes *simultaneously* with the melody notes.

## All together, now
To play the melody with the fingers, rest stroke, and simultaneously play a bass part with the thumb, free stroke, requires an unfamiliar combining of two familiar techniques. Don't be surprised to find that the sum of the parts is harder to play than it is to play each part separately. Don't be surprised if your mind tells your right hand fingers *and* thumb to play *only* free *or* rest strokes together. It is easier to do that. Resist the temptation, and remember to use the fingers, *rest* stroke; thumb, *free* stroke. If you let your fingers temporarily get by with free strokes, I can practically guarantee that later they will balk at playing rest strokes. If you can pat your head and rub your stomach at the same time, you certainly can learn to play simultaneous free and rest strokes...

Start with this easy open string exercise, carefully monitoring your right hand movements. Keep your thumb well out away from your fingers, or they will collide. Persist!

Etude Nine, *The Persistence of Gershwin,* based on the chord changes of *I Got Rhythm* (George and Ira Gershwin), is in this style. Bass notes are chord tones with half or whole note values. The intervals formed by the combination of the bass note and the melody note played with it are familiar, with the exception of sevenths and tenths, which will be taken up in Etude Twelve (p.69).

**Further exercises and supplementary material**
Continue the sit-on-an-accompanying-note-and-move-the-melody exercises you did earlier, now with the bass played simultaneously and more frequently. Make up routines through harmonized scales, cycle of fifth patterns, chromatic chord changes, etc. Arrange some, and improvise others. In fingering, go for flexibility and articulation of melody notes, which usually means avoiding barring except when necessary. Expertise in sensing coming-up left hand fingering takes years.

There are few books on this subject. Did I mention *Harmonic Mechanisms...* I think I did. There are wonderful models of single note accompaniments, fingerstyle, in the Bach cello and violin partitas, sonatas, and suites which have been transcribed for classical guitar. For the most part, these are the violin or cello single lines with the addition of bass notes. Beg and borrow from such arrangements, and if you steal, give credit. Do it—you can't invent It All.

**Tips**

**More bass in your bass—Part I: Change the strings**
If you like even more depth in your bass lines and would like to actually play notes below low E, here are some ideas on how to give your guitar the range of an electric bass.

Replace the fifth and/or sixth string(s) with string(s) tuned an octave below the standard tuning. Short scale electric bass strings, G and D will be a good bet for guitar A and E strings. D'Addario makes a George Van Eps-inspired A for the 7-string guitar which you might like for your A. Tuning peg holes, bridge saddles, and tail pieces will need minor modification for the thicker strings.

Now *that's* depth. But before you modify your instrument, remember that the notes you play on the fifth and sixth strings will *always* be an octave below, and such simple situations as playing a chromatic run from first to sixth string will not be possible anymore. Everything takes a dramatic plunge an octave downward after the fourth string. Is that okay with you?

This lowered string setup makes a good accompanying instrument for backing up a singer when you are the only accompanist–especially in oom-pah kinds of music. And, if you have a spare guitar, you could set it up for that special occasion. Don't try it on nylon stringed instruments.

# The Persistence of Gershwin

59

| Etude Ten: | *Montuna Tune* |
|---|---|
| Concept: | Repeated bass figures as accompaniment to melodic line |
| Technique: | Right hand: *a* plays bass; *i, m, a* play melody |
| | Left hand: no new movements |

## Further independency of lines

In most ways *Montuna Tune* is easier than much of the previous material in this book. There is one major exception. The bass line, being either one of two figures, is constantly repeated. Neither figure is difficult for the left hand, since both use open strings only. What *is* difficult is playing the *rhythm* of the bass figure together with rhythmic portions of the melody. You need to know what the rhythms of both parts sound like separately so that you can at least imagine what they sound like together in your mind's ear. Play them separately, first, and then together, very slowly. Then work at it as you would anything else.

I've called this Etude *Montuna Tune* because it has a Latin type of repeated bass figure, and a loose sort of improvisation. It starts with a quote from the folk song, *All the Pretty Little Horses,* and reaches a climax at the end of section two of the Etude. Section three is a tapering off and fading out, with a return to the bass figure in part one.

## Further exercises and supplementary material

Repeated bass figures occur most often in Latin, rock, and some jazz fusion music, so if this style appeals to you, seek it out.

This piece could conceivably be attached as a second chorus of *All the Pretty Little Horses,* a piece I arranged for *Solo Jazz Guitar,* an earlier book of solo jazz guitar pieces "in the styles of". It makes a good companion for this book.
Mel Bay is the Publisher.

### Tips

### When in groups...

The stress in this book is on unaccompanied fingerstyle jazz (self-accompanied, really) guitar, but everything in here can be applied in group situations too. About the only thing you need to be aware of is not to step on the toes of the other players in your group—particularly the bass player, who would like to contribute *his* lines without fighting the bass lines you will be capable of playing. Be judicious and put yourself in the places of the other members of your group. Play "group guitar" instead of solo guitar with your new concepts and techniques.

# Montuna Tune

63

| Etude Eleven: | *Blues For Howie* |
| --- | --- |
| Concept: | Single line melody accompanied by walking bass |
| Technique: | Right hand: *p* plays bass line while *i–m, a* play melody |
| | Left hand: constant shifting and long stretches, with even more independence of fingers |

### The walking bass

Today, even in the midst of the varieties of jazz fusion, the predominant way of playing string bass is still the *walking line* effect which originated in the swing era. The bass "walks" through the chord changes in basic four-to-the-bar rhythm, outlining the harmonic movement for the soloist to hear. In addition, if the bassist is really skillful, his line is a melody by itself, a counterpoint to the melody the soloist is improvising.

This walking bass line concept, when done on the guitar, is a sort of two-instruments-played-at-once effect. Because of the constant quarter note bass rhythm it's almost as difficult to improvise such a bass line *with* a lead line as playing two instruments at once! My advice is to pre-arrange a few choruses or memorize a few standard walking bass modules, or sections, so that you will still have part of your concentration left for the top improvised line.

This style makes more demands on your left hand than anything so far mentioned in this book. Two lines at once means that there is a relentless playing of two note intervals, most of them large, with constant shifting. The right hand is basic *i, m* and *a*, for melody, with *p*, playing bass, as in Etude Nine, *The Persistence of Gershwin.* The main differences are 1) the top melody and bass line are confined to higher and lower areas to dramatize the "two instrument" effect and 2) the bass is constant.

The best way to come up with good bass lines is to listen to what bass players play when they walk. Listen to how they use chord tones, passing tones, chromatic and scale steps, skipwise movements, etc. Listen also to guitar players who comp and play bass lines when there is no bass player in the situation. If you now are doing this, you are already in the ballpark. If not, you might start out practicing walking bass lines along with a whole note on top; then a half note; then quarter notes, and even work up to eighth notes. This would look like the illustration below, based on the bass line in measures 19-23 of *Blues for Howie.*

## Supplementary material

Bass books which show walking jazz lines will help you examine this concept. Two are *Contemporary Bass Solos* and *Studio and Stage Band Bass Studies*, both by Earl Gately (Mel Bay, Pub.). There is one especially delightful fingerstyle jazz/pop guitar method which has much material on the bass line as applied to fingerstyle guitar, and that is *The Howard Morgen Guitar Method for Fingerstyle Jazz and Popular Guitar, Vols. I and II*, by Howard Morgen (Big 3, Pub.). Howie was the first fingerstyle jazz player I heard in person, and his use of the walking bass line influenced my adding it to my solo guitar playing. Also, once again, *Harmonic Mechanisms, Vols. I, II and III*, by George Van Eps (Mel Bay, Pub.) contains a plethora of work related to two and more moving lines.

Tips

**More bass in your bass—Part II: Using an octave divider and adding a pickup**

With the invention of octave dividers, having a choice of *tessitura* (range) is only a matter of stepping on a foot switch. Again, I will presume that you want the low A and E strings as the octave-below strings. Install a small pick-up, such as a Fender Precision bass pick-up, positioned so that it is under *only* the lower two strings.

You will need a separate wiring rig, jack, and cord for this pick-up, or wire it into your existing rig and use a stereo cord with a "Y" at the outgoing end.

Now: plug the cord for this pick-up into the octave divider and set the octave divider control at the sub-octave position. Remember that an octave divider is a mono signal processing device, so one note at a time is the rule. Sub-octave or normal octave is now available at a foot tap.

Even in the sub-octave only mode you will still hear the normal pitch of the fifth and sixth strings *along with* the processed signal an octave lower. That's because your normal six string pick-up is also producing the natural pitch sound of A and E. If you don't want this, you can reposition your normal pick-up so that it covers the first four strings only, and always use the Precision bass pick-up as the bottom end pick-up, with or without the octave divider. On my guitar I have two Precision bass pick-ups near the neck, staggered very similarly to the bass pick-up position on an electric bass. Together they are my front pick-up.

If the aesthetics of the jerry-rigged look of this added pick-up bothers you, you can find a custom pick-up shop to build a split pick-up with a four string and a two string bobbin, end-to-end. It could replace your present pick-up, and would need a stereo cord and a mono/stereo switch. Make sure the customizer knows what he's doing.

About as expensive as a custom made pick-up is a hexaphonic pick-up, originally designed for use with guitar synthesizers. This pick-up has six wires coming from it, each corresponding to a string, and can be joined up in any configuration you'd like. See an electronics person for this job, too.

# Blues for Howie

| | |
|---|---|
| **Etude Twelve:** | *It Could Happen* |
| **Concept:** | Using chord partials, sevenths, tenths and sixths as accompaniment |
| **Technique:** | Right hand: more use of *a* in melodic work as *p-i-m* play chord tones |
| | Left hand: holding chord partials as lines move above them |

## Accompanying a melody with sevenths below

Fingerstyle playing makes major and minor sevenths available for accompaniment. Since jazz harmony can be said to begin with seventh chords, this is an important addition to the accompaniment devices introduced so far.

Here is an example of *single note* accompaniment with the interval of a seventh being formed between the bass note and first melody note of each chord change. *Since sevenths, alone, do not state major or minor tonality, the crucial major or minor third of the triad of each seventh chord is included in the melody.*

## Two note accompaniment with sevenths

This is a sample of sevenths used in *two note* accompanying. Once again, the crucial tonality-determining third is included in the melody corresponding to each chord.

## Accompanying a melody with tenths below

Thirds plus an octave make up tenths. While thirds are commonly used in close harmony with the melody (see *Ragtime Thirds,* Etude Thirteen), the octave lower separation turns thirds into the much lower tenths, which are considered bass notes. They can be played fingerstyle, only. In the example below, the major or minor tenth is enough to imply a major or minor chord. The melody as written fits within the framework of the minor, dominant, and major seventh indicated, but is lacking the additional coloration of the major or minor seventh interval. How could you rework the melody to include the complete chord? Remember that the perfect fifth of each of these chords is not crucial to the chord sound.

## Two note accompaniment with mixed sevenths and tenths

*It Could Happen,* Etude Twelve, is an improvised chorus based on the changes of *It Could Happen to You* (Jimmy Van Heusen and Johnny Burke), and the accompaniment is entirely sevenths and tenths. First, here is a sample of mixed sevenths and tenths as accompaniment.

**Further exercises and supplementary material**

You need to become facile in pulling out of your memory bank the fingerings of seventh and tenth intervals, so practice scales in those intervals, both horizontally and vertically on the fret board. Then noodle and doodle with one and two note seventh and tenth accompaniments to single line material you are already familiar with. Then mix and match with other accompanying devices. Listen to pianists who use tenths in accompaniment, such as Art Tatum, Teddy Wilson, or any current day pianists who are recreating this earlier style of piano playing.

**Tips**

**Something obvious about strings**

If you want the feel of your guitars to be as similar to each other as possible, don't forget the string factor. I learned about this the hard, expensive way.

A few years ago, I decided to have the *neck* of my L-5 widened to feel the same as my classical guitar neck, and asked my customizer (the late Jimmy DeSerio) to make it identical. When he finished the job, I picked it up, felt the strings, and accused him of being in error. The strings felt much wider apart than on my classical. We measured it. It was exactly the same. Then I noticed that the wound string spacing didn't feel different, it was the spacing of the top three strings that felt too wide. And then dismal enlightenment struck me: I had forgotten that unwound *steel* strings are *much* thinner than unwound *nylon.*

If the nut and bridge of a steel string instrument are notched with the same spacing as a nylon, the result will be that it will feel *much* wider —uncomfortably so, since a nylon string guitar is wide to begin with.

So, if you want the spacing of your steel string instrument to *feel* like a nylon, have the steel remade to somewhat narrower dimensions. How much narrower? You can begin by stringing up a classical guitar with silk and steel strings, *tune* it about a third below normal (for safety), and get a feel for how much is *too* wide, and figure from that.

By the way, if you want the top three strings of your current steel string instrument to feel more like a nylon, consider using a black nylon tape wound electric set first, second and third (D'Merle/D'Angelico makes them). Don't use the bottom three, as wound *steel* basses feel more like wound *nylon* basses than *tape wound* basses do. Please note that the use of these nylon tape wound strings didn't make the classical guitar spacing on my L-5 feel much closer together. Jimmy had to redo the neck. If I had been clairvoyant, I would have used the too-wide L-5 neck for my first seven string guitar...

71

# It Could Happen

| Etude Thirteen: | *Ragtime Thirds* |
| --- | --- |
| Concept: | Harmonization of melody in thirds, with lower bass note accompaniment |
| Technique: | Right hand: *i-m* and *m-a* play thirds as *p* plays bass |
| | Left hand: playing constant thirds accompanied by simple bass part |

Thirds as single note accompaniment to melodic lines was covered earlier in Etude Six. The use of thirds as a sustaining bass note, on top of which the melody rides, was illustrated in that section. This Etude illustrates a different use of thirds.

## Harmonizing the melody in thirds

Because of our cultural heritage, most of us grew up hearing *melodies harmonized in thirds.* As a normal child participating in group singing situations, I "faked" harmony in thirds long before I knew anything about music theory. If you did, too, it should be quite easy for you to track a melody with thirds on the guitar. Of course, it is easier to *conceive of* and *hear* thirds than it is to actually *play* them on guitar, so if you haven't been using scales harmonized in thirds as part of your daily routine, now is the time to begin.

## Right hand fingering of thirds alone

Two good ways of fingering thirds are illustrated below. Both are based on the simple principle that, all else being equal, alternating fingers is a better way than repeating fingers.

## Fingering thirds accompanied by a single bass note

Thirds plus a bass note are best handled this way:

*Ragtime Thirds* is an original tune in the style of the earliest days of jazz piano. Typically, ragtime melodies were harmonized in thirds, just as this tune has been.

## Further exercises and supplementary material

Take any familiar melodies and practice harmonizing them in thirds. Make sure you use the appropriate major or minor third which the chord progression and diatonic harmony demand. Occasionally you might need to use a fourth or fifth below a particular melody note so that the harmony will retain its integrity.

If you like ragtime guitar, you will enjoy the Scott Joplin arrangements by Tommy Flint in *Country Ragtime Guitar* (Mel Bay, Pub.). To see how ragtime piano arrangements can be scored for guitar, try working with *Matt Dennis Plays Scott Joplin,* by Matt Dennis (Mel Bay, Pub.).

### Tips

### More on fingernails

Now that your right hand nails are long enough to use, here's how to keep them that way.

Coatings:  Unless you are blessed with nails as strong as walrus tusks, you will need some help to keep them from damage—especially in the winter. Clear nail polish or any of the varieties of nail hardener similar to nail polish are good for  damage protection, but they don't protect the *tips* from wearing or make the nail itself any stronger since they don't join *with* the nail. *Protein nail conditioners* join with the nail, don't have a gloss (if gloss bothers you), and can be had at any cosmetic counter.

Repairs: Cracks and tears can be fixed with cyanoacrylate glues, that most wonderful and most horrible stuff. I've never gotten it in my eyes but I have glued my index finger to my thumb once. Don't laugh—I wouldn't wish that experience on anyone. So be *very* careful. Airplane glue or other quick (but not *so* quick) drying glues will work fairly well, and are much safer. Then layer over the mended nail with one of the coatings mentioned above.

Replacements:  There are several brands of powder and liquid mix-and-paint-on-build-a-nail kits. After some getting used to, during which you inadvertently build Pterodactyl claws, you can build fine replacement nails. I use this method a lot, and keep a kit around for my students. In the winter I routinely put a thin coating of this stuff on my nails as general protection.

I've also grafted left hand thumb nail tips onto broken right hand thumb nail stubs.

As I sit here and write this it occurs to me that I rarely have broken nail problems any more, and it isn't that I have nails of steel. When I first began fingerstyle guitar I sort of hacked away at the strings with my nails. Most broken nail accidents happened *while* playing guitar. I didn't have the finesse needed to gently stroke a string. After a number of years I gradually turned my karate attack into tai chi. It will happen to you, too—stay with it, and in the meanwhile use the above suggestions.

# Ragtime Thirds

| Etude Fourteen: | *Show Me the Way to Go Sixths* |
| --- | --- |
| Concept: | Sixths as accompaniment to melody, and harmonization of melody in sixths, with lower bass note accompaniment |
| Technique: | Right hand: *p-i* and *p-m* play sixths alone, or *i-m* and *i-a* play sixths as *p* plays bass |
| | Left hand: playing constant sixths accompanied by simple bass part |

## Sixths as sustaining bass notes, played fingerstyle

In Etude Seven sixths-as-bass-note-accompaniment was touched upon. The use of sixths played on *adjacent* strings is quite limited because of the long stretch needed.

When sixths are played fingerstyle—with a skipped string in between the upper and lower note—they are *very* useful.

Here are two new improvised versions of a section of the chord progression of *It Could Happen.* In both examples, sixths as accompaniment are mixed with sevenths and tenths. This is a more likely happening than the continual use of any one interval as the only accompaniment. Sometimes there is a single lower note and sometimes there are two. It is common for the density of accompaniment to vary.

79

## Harmonization of the melody in sixths

Sixths can be used like thirds, in continual harmonization of the melody. They are another familiar and "natural" sounding harmony to even the untrained ear.

## Right hand fingering of sixths alone

Sixths alone can be fingered either of the two following ways:

Country-funk jazz is full of sixths, and it is this style I have used in *Show Me the Way to Go Sixths*, a solo based on the chord changes of *Show Me the Way to Go Home* (Irving King).

## Further exercises and supplementary material

As you did with thirds, take familiar lines and harmonize them in diatonic sixths, being careful to use the appropriate major or minor sixth and to make adjustments with the use of other intervals if the use of sixths creates a clash.

Both the Van Eps books and many of the country style books of Tommy Flint, mentioned earlier, have exercises and pieces with sixths.

| Etude Fifteen: | *Will You Remember?* |
|---|---|
| Concept: | Constant four-to-the-bar chords used as rhythmic accompaniment to the melodic line |
| Technique: | Right hand:  damping chords while allowing melody to ring |
| | Left hand:  repeating chords as melody moves |

## Chunk, chunk, chunk, chunk

The effect of rhythm chords accompanying four beats to the measure is what this style is all about. The chords can have as many as four notes or as few as two. It's not important. As accompaniment, keep them softer than the melody, which is most often the top note.

I call this style the Freddy Garner or Green Erroll effect, using the Count Basie rhythm guitarist Freddy Green and the late pianist Erroll Garner as my sources. As to whether it was rhythm guitarists (or banjoists) who influenced certain pianists' left-hand four-to-the-bar accompaniment, or vice-versa, I'll defer to the jazz historians. We fingerstyle soloists have it now!

You can phrase the chords:

1)  Long

2)  Short

3)  Varied

No articulation other than plucking.

Damp or shorten the sound of the right hand fingers on the strings in anticipation of the next chord pluck (just the thing which you would normally avoid).

Alternate long and short.

## Voicing

The chords in Etude Fifteen are voiced mostly in root position, but you can voice them otherwise— especially when using this style and playing with a bassist. Do keep the voicing fairly close, and don't go for exotic bass line counterpoint, for that's not the mark of this particular mode.

## Pre-arranged or improvised?

The more simple the melody, the easier it is to keep the four-to-the-bar going. In this style it is easier to pre-arrange an accompaniment to a melody than to use on the spot improvisation. Improvisation is hard because so many fingers (and your mind) are committed to keeping the chords going that the single note improvisation ends up being whatever is *left over after* the chord accompaniment is formed. That's backward thinking, and improvisation suffers if done this way.

*Will You Remember* is based on the harmony of *I Remember You* (Johnny Mercer and Victor Schertzinger).

In order to focus your attention on the accompaniment, the chord stems are generally pointing downward. It might benefit you to go through the piece playing these accompanying chords only, then the melody only, and then both together.

**Further exercises and supplementary material**

Since this four-to-the-bar accompaniment of Etude Fifteen can be thought of as an imitation of the style of the late Erroll Garner, seek out any of his many recordings. There is a book of transcribed solos of his: *The Erroll Garner Songbook*, arranged by Sy Johnson *(Cherry Lane Music Co., Inc., Pub.)*.

There is a whole world of jazz piano books which relate very much to solo jazz guitar. Some good ones are:

*Jazz Piano Styles by Matt Dennis,*
*Blues Piano Styles by Matt Dennis,*
*Jazz Exercises for Piano by Paul Smith,*
*Piano Improvising by Wilfred Adler,*
They are all published by Mel Bay Publications.

 Tips

**A guitar is a guitar is a guitar**

As I mentioned above, there is a lot that can be learned about solo jazz guitar arranging by studying piano music.

And this business of chasing piano sounds can be overdone.

One of the reasons I was dazzled and seduced by solo jazz guitar, some fifteen years ago, was that so much music could come from a single guitar. "It sounds like a piano," was my reaction. So I began finger-style guitar in an effort to sound as much as, as big as, as good as, as pianistic as a piano.

I wasn't alone in my feeling that a guitar is some sort of fretted piano. Chapman invented his Stick and Van Eps added his seventh string in order to sound more like a piano.

It took me a while to realize that a guitarist playing the guitar could be compared to a peculiar sort of pianist who, in order to play piano, must press the piano keys down with one hand and at the same time reach inside the piano and pluck the corresponding strings with the other. Of course, pianists aren't hampered in that way. Just guitarists. So I would *never* sound "just like a piano." I went through a period of feeling helpless about the situation, until one day, in my effort to sound like keyboard synthesists, I tried a guitar synthesizer. Immediately I rejected it and embraced the guitar once again. It wasn't that I didn't like what it added. It was what it removed: all the uniqueness of the guitar sound. I realized then that in my effort to do what pianists do and sound like pianists sound, I had lost touch with the specialness of the guitar.

It's not surprising to me that I now play my acoustic instruments more than I did before that crucial experience. Now I enjoy even more the textures, slides, slurs, pluckiness, vibratos, strums, bent notes, and all the other qualities special to the guitar. Even string buzzes and mis-fretted notes!

# Will You Remember?

| Etude Sixteen: | *Luna Night Stream* |
|---|---|
| Concept: | The jazz waltz style |
| Technique: | Right hand: outside/inside chord plucking (*a* and *p*, followed by *m* and *a*) |
| | Left hand: no new movements |

## Outside/inside the jazz waltz

The jazz waltz is a "natural" for fingerstyle guitar, as the configuration of the fingers of the right hand works wonderfully to produce this basic rhythm:

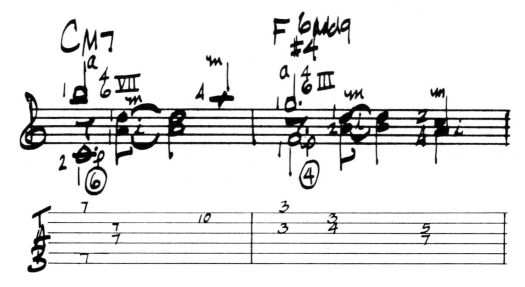

I call this the *outside/inside* plucking pattern, as two outside digits, the *p* and *a* fingers, pluck first, followed by the two inner digits: the *i* and *m* fingers. Commonly the *a* and *p* produce the melody and bass notes, using rest and free strokes, respectively, and are followed by the *i* and *m*. Most of the time the *a-p* combination, coupled with the *i-m*, form a four note chord. Examine this etude and you will see this device used more than any other.

## About the harmony

If you like the harmony in this piece, analyze the chord voicings measure by measure. The symbols are fairly comprehensive. Look for use of upper partials (ninths, elevenths, thirteenths), altered chords (Major #4 especially), and intervals in seconds.

## Fingering

As right hand fingering situations repeat themselves in these Etudes, there will be less notation of them. Already you have come a long way–especially if you have been working on supplementary material. The first half of this piece has been fingered. The second half doesn't contain anything not in the first half, so it has been left undigited. I encourage you to write the fingering in, if it helps.

*Luna Night Stream* is based on the harmony of *Moon River* (Henry Mancini and Johnny Mercer).

## Further exercises and supplementary material

Examine the jazz waltzes you have played with a pick until now, and rearrange them in the outside/inside method described at the beginning of this section.

There are no guitar solo books with only jazz waltzes, but there is usually at least one jazz waltz in most of them. Examine the Lenny Breau inspired arrangement of *Emily,* in *Chet Atkins Note-For-Note,* by Chet Atkins (Guitar Player, Pub., Mel Bay, Dist.), and *The Boy Next Door,* in *Contemporary Moods for Classical Guitar,* by Laurindo Almeida (Robbins Music Corp., Pub.).

# Luna Night Stream

# PART THREE: ALL THINGS CONSIDERED, COMBINING ALL OF THE CONCEPTS AND TECHNIQUES INTRODUCED

This last section consists of Etudes using all of the concepts and techniques presented in parts One and Two of this book. I wrote them as freely as I could, without restricting any of them to being an illustration of any one device. My desire is that by now you, too, are well on your way to having your self come through the music freely, and vice versa, without too many mental machinations.

## Other right hand possibilities

As you are aware, I have been stressing classical guitar right hand technique as sacrosanct. It's because the classical position is about as deeply formal, "fingery," and as different as one can get from pick style playing. I feel that when it is time for you to give fingerstyle a try, you might as well put down the pick and go full tilt with the fingers. And now that you have had an experience of playing *totally* "legitimate" fingerstyle, here are some variations. You probably know and may even use parts of these other possibilities. Something can be said for all of them.

## Variations of basic classical techniques:

a) Basic classical technique with the exception of using a pattern of *a-m-i* (or the reverse) to play single lines.

b) *Zone* playing, which I call the style of assigning right hand fingers systematically to the six string arena. In this system, *p-i* alternately plays linear material on the sixth and fifth strings, *i-m* plays material on the fourth and third strings, and *m-a* plays material on the second and first strings. There will naturally be some overlapping of assignments. The *e* finger could also be entered into the picture for some *a-e* work. Good luck on *that*.

c) Basic classical technique played with fingers and a *thumb pick.* This style has the advantages of strict classical technique *and* the advantages of playing single note lines in an almost-flatpicking manner. Naturally, folks who would use this technique are apt to have been flat pick or thumb pick players originally.

d) Pick *and* fingers. At first glance, this is the most natural and the best quick solution for flat pickers who want to play fingerstyle material. However, there are two big problems with pick and fingers:1) The *e* finger substitutes for the *a* finger. Quite simply, the *e* finger is not nearly as useable as the *a* finger. Worse, the *i* finger, since it holds the flat pick along with the thumb, is totally out of commission as an independent player. 2) *Thinking* in the manner a fingerstyle player thinks is very rare for flat pickers who use pick and fingers. All the ones I know use pick and fingers to play what could essentially be played with pick alone. The texture is different, but the concept isn't. So, if you do use pick and fingers, and want to play solo jazz guitar, make an extra effort to make what you play "fingery." You couldn't go wrong by working on some classical guitar material, played with pick and fingers, for the "fingery" concepts are the same as fingerstyle jazz guitar.

e) Palming a flat pick when playing fingerstyle, and then quickly flipping out the flat pick whenever quick linear material comes up because you never got your *i-m* together. I won't even lower myself to comment on that. Well, conscience demands that I do... *Of course* I tried that when I first began fingerstyle. I even drilled a hole in the pick and tied it on my finger with a rubber band. In the time it took me to find out all the ways that wouldn't substitute for getting my *i-m* together, I could have gotten my *i-m* together.

f) "Invisible flat picking." Basic classical technique, except for linear sections, when you hold your thumb against your index finger *as though* you are holding a flat pick. Using your index fingernail as a pick, pick those long single note sections. Open your hand for multiple string playing and general fingerstyle work.

g) Untitled. Using a common household spoon, a feather boa, a plate of fried shrimp, grab the guitar by the tuning pegs, and...

As for myself, I use *only* fingerstyle to play solo jazz guitar, classical, flamenco, ragtime, some country, and some blues. I use a pick to play with when a category, style, or individual piece demands the traditional rhythm and/or lead pick played sound. Really, there is no championing of one over the other, and I strive to keep up with both. How about you?

### Etude Seventeen:  *Huggable You, Part II*

This Etude is a continuation of Etude Three, *Huggable You.* It has been left for this section, as it must be played with a variety of fingerstyle techniques. As such, it contains no right hand fingering which hasn't been mentioned in Part Two. The left hand work should look familiar.

Keep this Etude in a relaxed, slow walk feeling.

97

## Etude Eighteen:  *Starboy, Cont'd*

*Starboy, Cont'd* is the fingerstyle-only second chorus of the earlier *Starboy, Etude Eight*.

Since the first six measures are slow-medium be-bop, play the eighth note chords with a slight long-short syncopation. The measures immediately following have mostly sixteenth notes in the melody, and should be interpreted more evenly, just as they are written.

Notice that the accompaniment to the sixteenth note melody of these measures is sparser, being one or two notes, rather than the earlier two or three notes used to accompany a melody in eighth notes. The faster the tempo of the piece, or in double timing (sixteenth note) sections, the sparser the accompaniment need be.

98

## Etude Nineteen:    *How About Me?*

*How About Me?* is a chorus on the chord changes of *How About You?* (Ralph Freed and Burton Lane). Keep the tempo of this piece reasonable, or the continual chord accompaniment of some sections will become fatiguing.

## Etude Twenty: *It's a Beginning*

*It's a Beginning* is a slow ballad solo based on *We've Only Just Begun* (Paul Williams, Roger Nichols). It features lush chord effects until the bridge, where, as a change of pace, it charges abruptly into a quasi-country picking vamp. The last section returns to slower paced chords and arpeggiation at the end.

104

105

## Etude Twenty-one: *Love is Green*

I've saved *Love is Green* for the last Etude because it does happen to include just about every concept and technique presented in this book. As a summation, you might like to analyze the piece to see if you can identify what you have been working on. It will help you to have a variety of approaches at your command when you arrange or improvise solo jazz guitar.

*Love is Green* is based on the chord changes of *Love is Blue* (Andre Popp and Pierre Cour).

107

*Tips*
*About bravery*

This last tip is probably the only secret in this whole book. And as secrets go, there is nothing secret about this secret. It's just that it takes a whole book to become prepared to really hear it.

*Intention counts.* To play solo jazz guitar well you must have the conviction and express in your playing that your music is complete in itself. That if the New York Philharmonic was hired to back you up, it would just mean more musicians, not better music.

As a solo guitarist there is no place to hide, anyway, so you might as well share yourself fully. Make your playing say, "Here we are, here is my music, and for now, This Is It." Doing that inspires people, and *that*, at least for me, is acknowledgement beyond all other rewards.

*Alan de Mause*

*Everybody's Music Teacher*